EVEN GRUES GET FULL

THE FOURTH USER FRIENDLY COLLECTION

by J.D. "Illiad" Frazer

O'REILLY®

Beijing · Cambridge · Farnham · Köln · Paris · Sebastopol · Taipei · Tokyo

Even Grues Get Full
by J.D. "Illiad" Frazer

Printed in the United States of America.

Production Editor: Claire Cloutier
Cover Designer: J.D. "Illiad" Frazer
Interior Designer: Robert Romano

Printing History:
August 2003:   First Edition.

ISBN: 0-596-00566-0
(M)

To my father,
who was Gandalf to my Frodo when I was five.

Other books by Illiad:

User Friendly: The Comic Strip
Evil Geniuses in a Nutshell: A User Friendly Guide to World Domination
The Root of all Evil

ACKNOWLEDGMENTS

This has been consistently the most terrifying part of the book to write, because I'm always terribly afraid of forgetting someone, only to remember them the instant the book goes to press.

Given that, I apologize to all of those whom I forget to mention, although you do certainly deserve recognition for what you contributed. I'm just a cartoonist, not a ROM chip.

Kickstart, Nea, Dragonlady, and Nawft for their daily vigilance, without which the UF comment system would slide into the chaos of sewage we find on the Net almost everywhere.

Betsy at O'Reilly and my agent David for keeping my eye on the ball.

The production team at O'Reilly for yet another painless publishing experience.

Tom and Ken for inspiring me every Thursday night, whether they realize it or not.

Valaria for providing me with a family point of view when it is most needed.

WebDiva and Yohimbe for always, and I do mean always, keeping the faith.

Davey, for continuing to provide me with faith.

Pixie, because she's my cat and she'd kick my butt if I didn't mention her.

UFies around the world for their much appreciated support, both financial and—more importantly—moral.

And Gretchen. No words needed.

COLOPHON

The cover illustration for *Even Grues Get Full* was provided by J.D. "Illiad" Frazer. The cover was produced by Emma Colby using QuarkXPress 4.1. Robert Romano produced the interior layout, based on a series design by Alicia Cech, using QuarkXPress 4.1 and the Monotype Gill Sans font. Claire Cloutier was the production editor. Colleen Gorman and Laurie Petrycki provided quality control.

Each night, before I can fall asleep, I have to read. If my head hits the pillow before I've spent some quality time with a book, I can count on a night spent staring at the ceiling, tossing and turning until dawn. I think this habit was spawned in my childhood, when my parents would allow me to stay up past my bedtime, as long as I was reading.

Since I was heavily into science fiction, fantasy, and horror, I often ended up reading stories that stimulated my imagination, or intrigued my budding young mind, and it wasn't uncommon for me to stay awake long after the rest of the house had gone to bed. These days, when I get into bed, I am usually accompanied by my airport-equipped iBook, and I read online comics.

In preparation for writing this foreword, I've been reading User Friendly. This is really pissing off my wife, because while she's trying to fall asleep, I'm giggling like crazy, poking her arm, and saying, "Oh man, this is *so funny!*" The thing is, the number of times I have said, "Oh man, this is *so funny!*" is precisely equal to the number of times my wife has said, "I don't get it," and rolled over to go back to sleep. Let this be a warning to all you geeks out there, who are married to normals: when your beloved wife just wants to go to sleep, it is the absolute **worst** time to explain why Cthulhu saying, "You like that? So? What's my name? Say my name, Mortal!" is so damn funny.

When Illiad asked me to write this, I told him that I'd love to, but I had no idea what I'd say. "OMFG! J00Z3r PHr3NDLEE IZ TEH FUTAR!!11" isn't exactly the stuff forewords are made of, you know? He suggested that I share with the reader how UF has affected my life. That's something I can work with, so here we go.

As a longtime UF reader, I was thrilled when I found myself included in a story line where AJ and Mike are putting together a game. When they find their budget is just 76 cents and a bus transfer, they realize that there is just one actor whom they can call: yours truly. This was in response to a note I posted on my own web site, where I talked about how much I'd like to do a voice in a video game. (As of this writing, it's still the closest I've gotten.)

The strip unfolded, and some of my friends thought that I would be offended or even hurt by the good-natured ribbing Illiad was throwing my way. But I'm a nerd, and being lampooned by User Friendly was as cool as getting to go on away missions with Captain Picard, and he's all, "Oh, Wesley, you are such a brilliant young man! I'm so proud to have you on my ship!" And then some badass alien comes after him, and you totally whip out your phaser, and blast his face off before he can grab the captain! And when you go back on the ship, Counselor Troi is all, "Hey, Cadet Crusher, I hear you saved the Captain! You know, I never noticed how hot you are. Why don't you join me and Robin Lefler in the Holodeck? We've been working on a special . . . dance . . . that you'd, uh, enjoy." And then she winks and licks her lips and—

Sorry. I just reversed the polarity on this foreword. Old habits die hard. Let's try again.

Being in User Friendly was a dream come true. (That's what I was going for there, before the geekout happened.) Readers of my web site, *wilwheaton.net*, discovered a hilarious online comic strip about people just like them. UFies came to my site, and discovered that the guy who played space nerd Wesley Crusher was just like *them*. (Sadly, we haven't been able to unite the two communities into an all-powerful army, hell-bent on global domination and dissolution of the RIAA.)

This collection is for geeks like us. It's targeted squarely at our unique funny zones, well outside of the mainstream. My wife will probably read this foreword, but that's about it. She's never going to think rubbing balloons on Dust Puppy to generate static is as funny as I do. And that's precisely the way it should be. You're going to love this book. Just don't read it in bed while your wife is trying to fall asleep. Trust me.

Wil Wheaton
Pasadena, California

*Humor is the affectionate
communication of insight.*
— Leo C. Rosten

It's an odd thing being a cartoonist. People expect very specific things from you.

I don't mean the cartoon-a-day expectation. That's taken for granted and I cheerfully accept that obligation. What I mean is the expectation that you're somehow significantly different from the rest of the world, significantly different from the people who read your work. They take a big thick brush and paint an "S" on your chest (whether that stands for Superman or Simpleton I'm still uncertain) and then stand there and stare at you, expecting you to launch yourself off a springboard and take to the sky.

(I'm assuming the Simpleton would do this without a parachute or other device to prevent deceleration trauma.)

I have this recurring nightmare. I go to a lot of conventions, and I sign a lot of autographs. I live in fear of the day when I sit behind a table, signing books, and a fan comes up and enthusiastically says, "So, you're Illiad," to which I politely reply, "Why yes, yes I am." The fan simply stands there and watches me for a minute while I sit in embarassed silence. He breaks the quiet agony with, "Hunh. You're not so funny."

I can feel the goosebumps prickling across my back even now. Ghost memories of knives.

This nightmare doesn't come from nullspace. When you're asked to speak at conventions (and I've been doing that a lot lately) and you're a cartoonist, people expect you to be funny. When politicians speak, people expect them to lie. When tax attorneys speak, people expect to fall asleep. When priests speak, people expect to also fall asleep. Whether or not these expectations are deserved remains a subjective question.

But if you're a cartoonist, you had damn well better be funny when you speak, or it's back to writing for '70s sitcoms for you.

I had considered the classic "funny test words" limelighted by the mad geniuses of Monty Python: "Wankel Rotary Engine" and "Grunties" get a titter out of people, but only the first time if you don't have a English accent. Talking like I had a tongue numbed by novocaine also made people laugh, but again, only once. And then they pointed at you and spoke in hushed tones with each other. Something about chanting baleful words before Cthulhu's rising.

So it falls to the material, the content of the speech. I slave over the major points of every talk I do, and once I've done that, I'm good to go. But when I'm done, I realize that I had just written enough humor for a week's worth of comic strips. And most of the people at the speech are people who read UF, so I know I can't recycle the funny stuff.

Ah, cruel, cruel life.

But back to the expectation: a great many people seem to think that cartoonists cause people to laugh wherever they go. Nothing could be further from the truth. Most cartoonists I know are shrinking violets, nondescript and perfectly happy with hiding in the darkest shadow in the room, sipping on fruit punch. We (and I merely speak for those who agree with me) chose our medium of telling because we're stage cowards; we love that we can hide behind a keyboard, ink and paper, and Groucho Marx glasses. And best of all, cartoonists aren't asked to do speeches.

And so is created another myth. Since I started UF, I think I've done somewhere in the neighbourhood of a hundred talks. And the truth is, I kind of enjoy it.

So I guess cartoonists ARE funny all of the time, if you use the definition of "funny" that relates to strangeness. We are the tumbleweeds of contradiction and self-incrimination rolling across the desert of humanity, until we latch on to a sultan's sexy daughter who can support us in the manner which we expect.

I can hear women around the world laughing hysterically now. Guess I've done my job for the day.

J.D. "Illiad" Frazer
Vancouver, British Columbia
June 2003

FULLY COGNIZANT OF THE INHERENT PROPERTIES
OF THE '2001: A SPACE ODYSSEY' MONOLITH,
TWO GEEKS DELIVER A PACKAGE TO
A PLACE THAT SORELY NEEDS IT

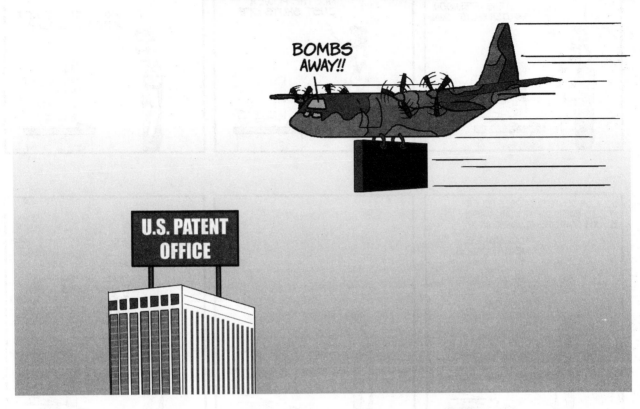

WHAT IF:
AOL TIME WARNER WAS A BUILDING COMPANY?

DEEP IN THE CONCRETE BOWELS OF A SECRET BUNKER, INFORMATION IS SIFTED, TRADED AND EMBELLISHED. *THE NERVOUS SYSTEMS OF THE FILM AND MUSIC INDUSTRIES MEET HERE AT A NEXUS, THE REPTILIAN BRAIN OF THE BIG MEDIA COMPANIES AS IT WERE.*

PART OF THE INFORMATION COLLECTION PROCESS INVOLVES A "HIGHLY DRIVEN TEAM OF SCRIPT-RUNNING JUVENILES."

OOOOH!

LEET!

ONE OF THESE "SRJS" COMES ACROSS *MIRANDA'S MOVIEOS* AND QUIETLY COMMUNICATES THE FIND TO HIS SUPERIORS.

D00DZ! F0UND 4N 0S H3R3 TH4T'11 ROCK YOUR WORLD!

♪ I'M TOO LEET FOR MY CAR TOO LEET FOR MY CAR TOO LEET BY FARRR ♪

SETTLE DOWN, DWORKMEYER. WHAT EXACTLY DID YOU FIND?

IT'S A NEW OS. IT DOES ALL THE FUNKY STUFF COMPUTERS DO IN THE MOVIES WE MAKE. Y'KNOW, LIKE THE 20-COLUMN SCREENS?

DOES IT NOW.

YEP.

SOMEBODY GET LEGAL ON THE PHONE!!

WHICH DEPARTMENT, PATENTS OR THREATS?

HAVING DISCOVERED MIRANDA'S MOVIEOS, THE SECRET OPERATIONS AND INTELLIGENCE DIRECTORS OF THE FILM AND RECORD INDUSTRIES CONFER TO DECIDE ON A COURSE OF ACTION...

SUE! PATENT! DEMAND!

AFTER MUCH DEBATE, THE SECRET PANEL DECIDES THAT THE ONLY ACTION THAT CAN BE TAKEN IS ONE WHICH GUARANTEES THEIR CONTINUED CONTROL...

SAME OLD, SAME OLD? LOOKS LIKE IT.

...AN ACTION THAT THEY'RE REASONABLY FAMILIAR WITH...

WE STEAL IT!

"ACQUIRE," OLD BOY. STEALING IS FOR CRIMINALS. WE'RE A MEGACORPORATION.

I'VE NOTIFIED COVERT OPS TO BEGIN THE ACQUISITION MISSION.

I HATE TO ASK, BUT WHY EXACTLY ARE WE TRYING TO ACQUIRE THIS "MOVIEOS?" IT DOESN'T COMPETE DIRECTLY WITH WHAT WE DO. NOR DOES IT INFRINGE ON ANY OF OUR INTELLECTUAL PROPERTY.

HAVE YOU CONSIDERED HOW IT MIGHT GIVE SOMEONE THE DANGEROUS **IDEA** THAT THEY **COULD** COMPETE DIRECTLY WITH US?

GEEZ. OPEN YOUR EYES. FINKLE.

THE MEGACONTENT INDUSTRY COVERT OPS TEAM SCOPES OUT THE TARGET, A SMALL, UNIMPOSING BUILDING IN THE HEART OF THE CITY...

Columbia Internet

THE TEAM LEADER SHOWS UR CONFIDENT THAT HIS UNIT IS PENULTIMATELY TRAINED AND ONE OF THE BEST EQUIPPED...

Columbia Internet

...OF COURSE, EVEN THE BEST CAN FORGET THE OCCASIONAL ITEM...

CEASE AND DESIST LETTERS?

CHECK!

OWNERSHIP WAIVERS?

CHECK!!

PENS?

UMMM...

Columbia Internet

THE TEAM PREPARES TO ASSAULT THE INNER REACHES OF THE TINY ISP...

YOU BOYS READY?

SURE.

GUESS SO.

WE AREN'T EVEN **IN** YET. WHY ARE YOU GUYS CROUCHING FUNNY?!

AND I AIN'T GETTING KICKED IN THE NARDS LIKE LAST TIME.

I NEED TO PEE.

11

FRIENDLY
the comic strip

UM...WHY ARE YOU DRINKING SO MUCH MILK?

BECAUSE WE'RE GONNA DO A LOUIS ARMSTRONG SONG.

SHHLLUP

(SUNG TO "WHAT A WONDERFUL WORLD" BY LOUIS ARMSTRONG)

I SEE CHEAP CPUS...
AND SOFTWARE THAT'S GREAT
AND MY MODEM CONNECTS...
AT TRUE 28.8
AND I THINK TO MYSELF..
...WHAT A WONDERFUL WORLD..

I SEE PEOPLE ON THE NET...
WHO ARE NICE AND NOT "LEET"
AND HARDWARE THAT NEVER...
BECOMES OBSOLETE
AND I THINK TO MYSELF..
...WHAT A WONDERFUL WORLD...

THE COLOURS OF THE IMAC...
SO PRETTY ON MY DESK
(THESE ARE COLOURS THAT ARE TASTEFUL
NOT ONES THAT ARE GROTESQUE)
I SEE ROUTERS SHAKIN' HANDS
SAYIN' "WHO THE HECK ARE YOU?"
BUT THEY'RE REALLY SAYING
"LET THE DATA FLOW THROUGH"

WOOO! GIVE HIM A TRUMPET!

BLUE SCREENS OF DEATH...
DON'T EXIST TO BETRAY
AND I DECIDE FOR MYSELF..
WHERE I WANT TO GO TODAY
AND I THINK TO MYSELF.
WHAT A WONDERFUL WORLD
YES. I THINK TO MYSELF.
WHAT A WONDERFUL WORLD...

KLIK
WHIRRR
KA-CHUNKA

IF YOU'RE DONE, LET'S GET BACK TO REALITY...

WELCOME TO DOTCOMBAT INC! I'M YOUR FRIENDLY H.R. MANAGER AND I JUST WANT YOU TO KNOW THAT WE'LL DO ALL WE CAN TO MAKE YOUR CAREER HERE WITH US AS PLEASURABLE AS POSSIBLE!

WE SEE THAT YOU HAVE A PULSE AND YOU LOOK GOOD IN A TIE. IS THERE ANYTHING ELSE YOU CAN TELL US TO HELP PLACE YOU IN POSITION BEST SUITED FOR YOUR EXPERIENCE?

NAKED...IN BED...WITH SMELLY...CODER...

AH! YES. WE HAVE A NEED FOR A GOOD PROJECT MANAGER!

AS THE RESCUE TEAM DEPARTS WITH STEF IN TOW, THEY STUMBLE ACROSS THE MPAA COVERT OPS BEER HALL...

HEY...I THINK THOSE ARE THE GUYS WHO NICKED STEF...

UH OH.

BRKKKKAAPAPAP APAPAPAPAPAPPA PAPAPAPAPAPAPP PAPAPAPAPPPAP APAPAPAPAP yearrgh!

THEY HAD NO GUNS AND NO TIES. WHAT'S YOUR EXCUSE THIS TIME?

I HAD AMMO.

AJ AND ERWIN SPIRIT AWAY WITH STEF, WHICH UTTERLY MADDENS THE MEGACORPORATION. THE COVERT OPS TEAM IS SENT OUT TO EXACT REVENGE.

GO GO GO GO GO!!

IF HE SCREAMS THAT IN MY EAR ONE MORE TIME, I'M GOING TO FEED HIM MY SHOTGUN STOCK.

THE TEAM IS TO BE PARACHUTED INTO THE TARGET ZONE, SO THEY BOARD THE CORPORATE C - 130 HERCULES...

GO GO GO GO GO!!!

THAT DOES IT.

SADLY FOR THE TEAM LEADER, HIS EXHUBERANT URGINGS MADE HIS TEAM TWITCHY. SO THEY ATE HIM. AND THERE WAS MUCH REJOICING.

YAAAAAAY

TAKING AFTER MOVIES SUCH AS NAVY SEALS, THE OPS TEAM DEPLOYS USING A HALO INSERTION (HIGH ALTITUDE LOW OPENING), A PARTICULARLY DANGEROUS AND COOL-SOUNDING METHOD OF PARACHUTING INTO ENEMY TERRITORY.

SADLY FOR THE OPS TEAM, WHICH PRIMARILY CONSISTS OF ACTORS AND NOT MILITARY PERSONNEL, THE PARACHUTES WERE NEGLECTED.

UH...

THUS WAS BORN THE HANO INSERTION, HIGH ALTITUDE NO OPENING, PARTLY NAMED AFTER THE SCREAMS OF REALIZATION.

HEY! NOOOOOOOOOO

YOU HEAR SOMETHING?

MMM...NOPE.

WHUMP

16

A LESS EXPENSIVE BUT JUST AS EFFECTIVE ALTERNATIVE TO A U.S. NATIONAL I.D. CARD.

WITH SUPERBOWL SUNDAY BEING TELEVISED EVERYWHERE, INCLUDING POWER-STARVED CALIFORNIA, SID ONCE AGAIN PROVES THAT TIMING IS **EVERYTHING**...

EARTHQUAKE NEAR REDMOND

FRIENDLY
the comic strip

HI FOLKS! MIKE FLOYD HERE. YOUR FRIENDLY NETWORK NEIGHBOUR-HOOD MANAGER!

THAT WOULD BE "FRIENDLY NEIGHBOURHOOD NETWORK MANAGER."

DYSLEXIA SURE CAN BLAZE A TRAIL TO PERSONAL HELL, CAN'T IT.

TODAY YOU LUCKY VIEWERS WILL BE THE FIRST TO SEE A BREAKTHROUGH IN COMIC STRIP TECHNOLOGY - 3D! HANG ON AND WATCH!

IN GLORIOUS 3D!!

THAT'LL SHOW 'EM THAT ILLIAD KNOWS HOW TO DRAW HANDS.

EXCEPT FOR THE FACT THAT YOU ONLY HAVE THREE FINGERS.

THAT WAS A PRETTY COOL COURSE OVER-ALL, WASN'T IT STEF?

YEAH, WHATEVER.

WONDER WHAT SID MEANT WHEN HE SAID A COMPANY WOULD DO BETTER WITH A MAGIC 8-BALL INSTEAD OF YOU FOR A NETWORK TECH.

YOU KEEP THAT UP AND YOUR OUTLOOK WON'T BE GOOD.

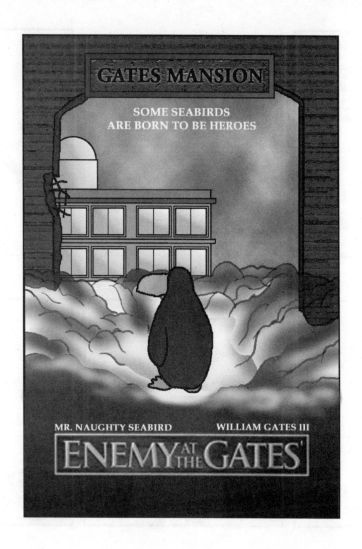

33

THE LOCATION OF CHOICE BY TACO BELL EXECUTIVES FOR THE "IF MIR HITS OUR TARGET, WE'LL GIVE EVERYONE IN THE U.S.A. A FREE TACO" PUBLICITY PLOY

HEADQUARTERS

UH...WHAT THE **HELL** ARE YOU?

CTHULHU. YOU MIGHT HAVE HEARD OF ME. I WAS SUPPOSED TO WAKE AND LAY WASTE TO THE WORLD WHEN THE STARS WERE "RIGHT". BUT I GOT KINDA ANTSY.

OH RELAX. I'M NOT HERE TO SMEAR THE WORLD. **UNLESS.** OF COURSE, YOU DECIDE THAT TUTORING ME IN XML IS **BENEATH** YOU.

OF COURSE IT'S NOT BENEATH ME ...ACTUALLY IT IS... NO!! IT'S NOT BENEATH ME!!

USER

FRIENDLY
the comic strip

Portrasber 4

ROTO-ROUTER 800

HEY. I'M HERE TO DO THAT "HISTORY OF EASTER" THING.

THAT'S GREAT, SID.

WANT US TO HOLD ON TO YOUR CHOCOLATE BUNNY FOR YOU?

SURE. BUT IF HE COMES BACK MINUS ANY BODY PARTS, I'LL BE SEEKING FLESH REPLACEMENTS.

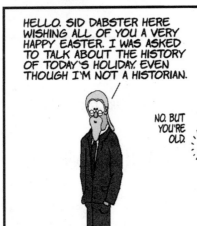

HELLO. SID DABSTER HERE WISHING ALL OF YOU A VERY HAPPY EASTER. I WAS ASKED TO TALK ABOUT THE HISTORY OF TODAY'S HOLIDAY. EVEN THOUGH I'M NOT A HISTORIAN.

NO. BUT YOU'RE OLD.

UM. ANYWAY. THE NAME EASTER COMES TO US FROM THE SAXON EOSTRE. GODDESS OF THE MOON. AND THE EASTER BUNNY COMES FROM THE RABBIT AS AN ANCIENT SYMBOL OF SPRING AND RENEWAL...

WHICH IS ALL REALLY BORING. YOU PEOPLE NEED TO STOP FRETTING ABOUT THE MEANING OF THE HOLIDAY AND JUST HAVE FUN! I PERSONALLY LOVE THE EASTER EGG HUNT!

THAT'S BECAUSE YOU CAN HIDE YOUR OWN EASTER EGGS, SID.

THE LATEST DIPLOMATIC SALVOES WERE EXCHANGED TODAY BETWEEN THE U.S. AND CHINA OVER THE HAINAN SPY PLANE INCIDENT. THE PLANE REMAINS IN THE POSSESSION OF CHINESE OFFICIALS DESPITE STRENUOUS OBJECTIONS ON THE PART OF THE U.S...

DEFENSE DEPARTMENT OFFICIALS ARE GRAVELY CONCERNED FOR THE INTEGRITY OF THE SECRET TECHNOLOGY FOUND ON BOARD THE US SPY PLANE...

HEH. DON'T THINK THEY NEED TO BE WORRIED ANYMORE.

WHY. WHAT DID YOU DO?

MEANWHILE, ON HAINAN ISLAND, CHINA...

NOW THIS IS INTERESTING. WONDER WHAT IT DOES.?

IT LOOKS LIKE A PAPER CLIP.

HELLO! YOU APPEAR TO BE RIPPING OFF TECHNOLOGY! CAN I HELP?

ONE OF THE H.P. LOVECRAFT ESTATE'S LESS SUCCESSFUL MERCHANDISING EFFORTS

WE HAVE TO GO TO CHINA AND EVACUATE CLIPPY.

WE WHAT?! WHY?

BECAUSE WHAT YOU DID WAS *MEAN* ERWIN. HOW COULD YOU BE SO UNTHINKING?

HM. GUESS YOU HAVE A POINT.

DARN RIGHT I DO. THE CHINESE DON'T DESERVE THAT KIND OF NASTINESS...

ERWIN AND DUST PUPPY BOARD A SHIP LEAVING FOR CHINA...

WHERE'D YOU GET THE TICK-ER TAPE?

UHM...

ERWIN!! GIVE ME BACK THE CABLE!!

...AND AS WORLDLY TRAVELLERS THEY SEEK OUT SHIPBOARD ENTERTAINMENT.

HELLO. ARE YOU THE CRUISE DIRECTOR? WE'RE LOOKING FOR A DISTRACTION TO WHILE AWAY THE TIME, LIKE SHUFFLEBOARD PERHAPS?

THEY'RE TROLLING FOR SHARKS OFF THE STERN. WANT TO GO HELP?

HMM. THAT DOES SOUND FAMILIAR.

THE CHIEF. THE V.C. BLOOD IN THE WATER.

AS DUST PUPPY WHILES AWAY THE TIME BY EXPLORING THE SHIP TO CHINA, HE DISCOVERS A TRAPDOOR TO A HOLD AND DESCENDS INTO THE DARKNESS...

WITH SOME SURPRISE, OUR HIRSUTE HERO DISCOVERS LIVING BEINGS HUDDLING IN THE DARKNESS...

WHO PRAY TELL ARE YOU?

LAID OFF TECH WORKERS! WE'RE GOING TO THE LAND OF RICE AND MONEY!

CHIK!

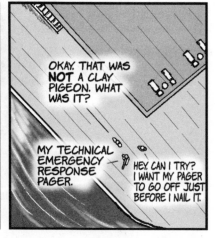

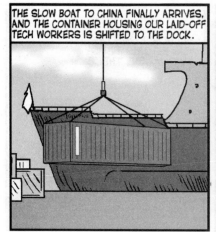

THE TOP FIVE REASONS WHY THE "TOMB RAIDER" MOVIE WILL BE A RAGING SUCCESS AMONG GEEK MALES

GOOD DAY EVERYONE. WE INTERRUPT THE CURRENT STORYLINE TO ADDRESS SOME FEEDBACK FROM THE VIEWERS REGARDING THE CARTOON YESTERDAY THAT FEATURED ANGELINA JOLIE AS LARA CROFT FROM "TOMB RAIDER."

GIVEN THAT THE RENDERING OF MS. JOLIE WAS CLOSER TO THAT OF AN ODDLY SHAPED TURNIP WITH A PERSIMMON FOR LIPS THAN A SEXY ACTION GODDESS, ILLIAD HAS TAKEN IT UPON HIMSELF TO LEARN THE LINE OF THE FEMININE FORM.

SO HOW LONG DO YOU FIGURE, ILLIAD? TWO, MAYBE THREE...

...DECADES.

WHILE PLAYING YOUR FAVOURITE FIRST-PERSON SHOOTER, IT HELPS THE EXPERIENCE IF YOU WEAR THE APPROPRIATE PANTS.

QUAKE III

RAINBOW SIX

CLIVE BARKER'S "UNDYING"

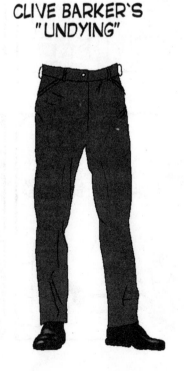

TIME-WARNER EMPLOYEES ARE TOLD TO USE AOL MAIL IN THE ONLY WAY THAT AOL KNOWS HOW

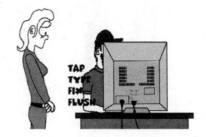

LISTEN, RICK. IN MY OPINION YOU BOTCHED THE WRAP-UP FOR VOYAGER. YOU HAD A CHANCE TO REALLY TUG AT OUR HEARTS BUT YOU BLEW IT.

HMMM.

BUT I'LL WATCH THE NEXT SERIES, BECAUSE I HAVE FAITH. JUST DO BETTER NEXT TIME. OKAY?

FAIR ENOUGH. SO..YOU DIDN'T THINK IT WAS INAPPROPRIATE FOR ME TO CALL YOU ABOUT THIS?

HECK NO. I RECOGNIZE THAT THE STAR TREK UNIVERSE HAS BEEN IN DIRE NEED OF TECHNICAL SUPPORT FOR DECADES.

HEY!!

I'M VERY GLAD I COULD HELP, RICK. BUT ONE LAST THING: YOU GUYS NEED TO WORK ON THE PREDICTABILITY A LITTLE.

PREDI-- HOW DO YOU MEAN?

OH COME ON. IF YOU WROTE A SERIES OF MYSTERY NOVELS INSTEAD AND USED THE SAME FORMULAS YOU DO IN STAR TREK, IT'D BE DISASTROUS.

ACTUALLY, WE JUST PUBLISHED A **WHOLE LINE** OF STAR TREK MYSTERY NOVELS...

THE PARTICLE-OF-THE-WEEK DID IT. IN ALL OF THEM.

OKAY YOU SICK LITTLE HAIRBALL. WHAT ON EARTH **IS** THAT THING?

IT'S A CTHIA PET, ERWIN AND I BROUGHT ONE BACK FROM CHINA.

ERWIN TRANSLATED THE INSTRUCTIONS. APPARENTLY YOU JUST ADD WATER AND IT GROWS TENTACLES AND STUFF. IT'S SUPPOSED TO MAKE A GOOD PET.

A PET, HUH? BET IT'LL GET ME CHICKS. SEE YA LATER, LOSERS.

ERWIN, YOU DIDN'T FORGET TO ADD THE WARNING ABOUT IT EATING MEAT DID YOU?

UM, WELL NO. I DIDN'T FORGET PER SE...

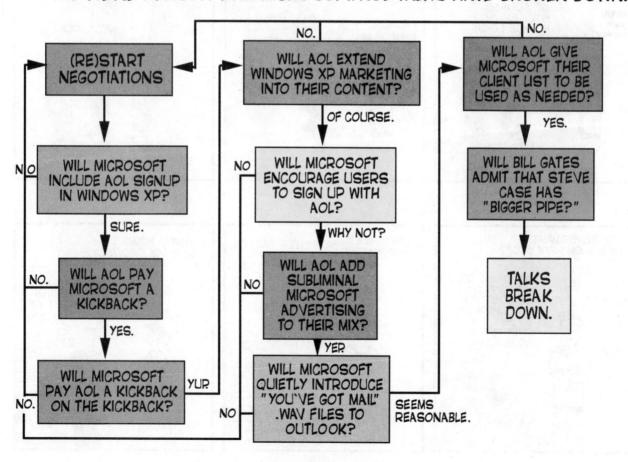

IN A RECENT INTERVIEW, MICROSOFT CEO STEVE BALLMER WAS QUOTED AS SAYING: "LINUX IS A CANCER THAT ATTACHES ITSELF IN AN INTELLECTUAL PROPERTY SENSE TO EVERYTHING IT TOUCHES."

THE MEDICAL RESEARCHERS AT BEAKER-BUNSEN TOOK UP THE CHALLENGE TO CAREFULLY DISSECT BALLMER'S STATEMENT. THEY DISCOVERED THAT THERE WAS INDEED MEDICAL PRECEDENT FOR CALLING LINUX A CANCER.

WE ASKED THEM WHAT THE MEDICAL EQUIVALENT WOULD BE FOR WINDOWS. "TOURETTE SYNDROME, OF COURSE," THEY REPLIED.

OKAY YOU LITTLE TWERPS. TELL ME HOW TO GET THIS THING OFF MY HEAD.

GRRR YUM MUNCH

OF COURSE STEF. ERWIN, PLEASE LOOK UP HOW THAT'S DONE.

SEARCHING...

IT SAYS HERE TO PUT A LENGTH OF LICORICE UP AND OUT YOUR NOSTRILS, AND THEN FLOSS VIGOROUSLY.

CHEW GNAW

HUNH. WELL, ANYTHING TO GET THIS SLUG CREATURE OFF ME.

YOU DIDN'T *ACTUALLY* LOOK ANYTHING UP DID YOU.

WELL, DUH.

HEY GUYS? WHAT'S GOING ON WITH STEF?

OH. ERWIN TOLD HIM TO FLOSS HIS NOSTRILS WITH LICORICE TO GET THE CTHIA PET OFF HIS HEAD.

ERWIN TOLD HIM **WHAT**?!!

BUT STEF SAID HE DIDN'T HAVE THE COURAGE TO DO IT HIMSELF.

THAT'S RIGHT. I SAID *VIGOROUSLY*.

WHAT IS IT WITH ME AND TUBES COMING OUT OF NOSES?

YEEEEOWCH!!

YE GODS! DON'T TELL ME STEF...

YUP. FLOSSED HIS NOSE. OR TRIED TO.

GAAAAH!!

HE KEEPS BREAKING OFF THE END THAT HE'S PULLING ON SO HE HAS TO REACH IN AND GET THE TIP OUT AGAIN.

AAAIIIEEEEEEEEEEE!

BUT WHY DOESN'T HE JUST PULL IT ALL OUT FROM THE OTHER END?

GUESS I COULD HAVE MENTIONED IT TO HIM.

WHO IS LEAVINK LICORICE LYINK AROUND? IS GOOD.

DID YOU FINALLY TELL STEF THE TRUTH ABOUT HOW TO GET RID OF THAT CTHIA PET?

YEAH. "CTHIA PET DOES NOT ENJOY BATTERY ACID." RIGHT OFF THE PACKAGING.

UH...STEF? YOU GOT THE CTHIA PET OFF YOUR HEAD?

UNH-HUH... SPRAYED... WITH... BATTERY... ACID...

OH DEAR. IT SEEMS, I LEFT OUT THE PART THAT SAYS "CTHIA PET WILL RUN FROM ACID AND HIDE IN YOUR PANTS."

EEP.

GRRR

SO. YOU INSTALLED LINUX ON YOUR MOM'S COMPUTER AND SHE WANTS TO GO BACK TO WINDOWS BECAUSE IT MAKES HER FEEL "MORE COMFY"?

YEAH. I EVEN DRESSED UP THE GUI TO LOOK LIKE THE WIN98 DESKTOP AND IT'S STILL NOT GOOD ENOUGH FOR HER.

HOW ABOUT SETTING UP A CRON JOB THAT REBOOTS THE MACHINE FOR HER EVERY DAY?

OOOH! AND SHE'LL NEVER KNOW THE DIFFERENCE!!

FRIENDLY
the comic strip

MIKE! THANKS FOR COMING BACK TO BIZEXPO. AND THANK YOU FOR AGREEING TO SPEAK AGAIN.

MY PLEASURE! I GUESS THE AUDIENCE REALLY ENJOYED MY TALK ON ETHICS FROM LAST TIME?

OH YES! YOU'RE THE BEST STAND-UP COMEDIAN WE'VE EVER HAD HERE.

LADIES AND GENTLEMEN. I'D LIKE TO INTRODUCE OUR FIRST SPEAKER. MIKE FLOYD. WHO LAST SPOKE HERE ON FEBRUARY 6, 1999. HE'S HERE TONIGHT TO PRE-EMPTIVELY ADDRESS CRAIG MUNDIE'S PHILOSOPHY ON...

AS GOD IS MY WITNESS. I **SWEAR** THIS SAYS "SHARED SORES."

YOU GOT IT **RIGHT** THIS TIME...

CHIEF. YOU WANTED TO SEE ME?

YES HILLARY. I NEED YOU TO FIND US SOME EXTRA OFFICE SPACE. IT'S GETTING CROWDED AROUND HERE AND I THINK IT'S TIME WE GAVE THE TECHS THEIR OWN OFFICE.

SURE...ANY PARTICULARS IN MIND? COST? LOCATION?

I DON'T CARE WHERE. JUST MAKE SURE IT HAS MINIMAL IMPACT ON OUR EXPENSES.

CAUTION: ABANDONED MISSILE SILO

RADIATION STUDIES LIVE-IN VOLUNTEERS WANTED.

AND YOU THOUGHT CEL PHONES IN CARS CAUSED THE MOST ACCIDENTS...

http://www.babe-alicious.com/

THIS LOOKS LIKE A NARROW EAST-WEST PASSAGEWAY. THERE IS A NARROW STAIRWAY LEADING DOWN AT THE NORTH END OF THE ROOM.

GUESS WE SHOULD GO WEST...

WE'RE NOW IN A SMALL ROOM WITH PASSAGES EAST AND SOUTH. AND A FORBIDDING HOLE LEADING WEST. BLOODSTAINS AND DEEP SCRATCHES MAR THE WALLS.

KEEP IT UP MAN, AND I'LL TEAR YOU A BIGGER "FORBIDDING HOLE."

MY TRAPDOOR SLAMS SHUT BEHIND ME...

ARCADE ANALOGIES

THE GPL:
PAC MAN

MICROSOFT'S PREFERRED
ARRANGEMENT:
ANY ARCADE GAME
THAT REQUIRES YOU TO
KEEP PLUGGING IN QUARTERS
REGARDLESS OF SKILL.

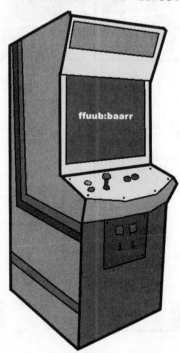

68

THE U.S. COURT OF APPEALS INADVERTENTLY AFFECTS THE ENGLISH LANGUAGE.

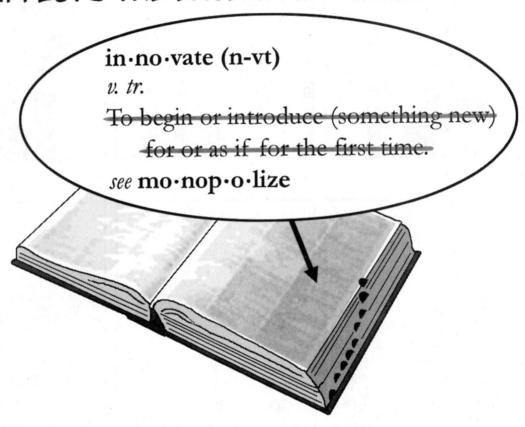

in·no·vate (n-vt)

v. tr.

~~To begin or introduce (something new)~~ ~~for or as if for the first time.~~

see mo·nop·o·lize

HEY MAN. YOU OKAY?

PEACHY. CONSIDERING THAT I JUST HAD SOME UNWANTED TECHNOLOGY INTRUSIVELY SHOVED UP ME DESPITE MY CRIES OF ANGUISH AND PLEAS FOR MERCY.

THE MISSILE. GREG.

OH. OKAY. I WAS JUST ABOUT TO SAY THAT MICROSOFT'S SMART TAGS HADN'T BEEN RELEASED YET.

HOLY ANTIQUES BATMAN! THERE'S SOME **SERIOUSLY** ANCIENT HARDWARE IN HERE.

YEAH. HEY! I DESIGNED AND OPERATED THIS!

YAH? SO WHAT EXACTLY IS IT?

WHY, ITS A PSEUDO-BABBAGE BOOLEAN ALGEBRA DEVICE THAT OPERATES WITH XOR, NOR AND NAND LOGIC GATES.

OKAY FINE. BUT WHAT DID IT **DO**?

IF I RECALL CORRECTLY, IT'S PRIMARY FUNCTION WAS TO PROVIDE ME ABSOLUTE JOB SECURITY.

SID! **PLEASE** BEINK CAREFUL! HAVE DROPPED REMOTE MISSILE LAUNCH **SWITCH** SOMEWHERE HERE. MISSILE IS HAVINK LARGE NUCLEAR WARHEAD...

DANG. THAT'S SERIOUS. I'LL HELP YOU FIND IT.

CHIKK

OH, SILLY ME. PLAYINK WITH CLICKER AT TIME LIKE THIS...

WIBBLE.

CHIKKA CHIKKA

OPS 4

COMRADES. AM FINISHED INSTALLINK MISSILE CONTROLS. NOW MUST BE RUNNINK SIMULATIONS FOR A TIME, DA?

OPS 4

SO, MEANWHILE MUST LEAVE REMOTE LAUNCH SWITCH IN CARE OF SOMEONE. IS WERY GRAVE RESPONSIBILITY. HAVINK TWENTY KILOTON YIELD AT FINGERTIPS.

EVIL GENIUSES. CHAPTER SEVEN. ATTRACT MINIONS WITH COOL ELECTRONICS THAT BLOW STUFF UP.

4

ME! ME! OOH! ME!

OH PLEASE! OH PLEASE!

THE LATEST HORROR MOVIE FOR INTEL

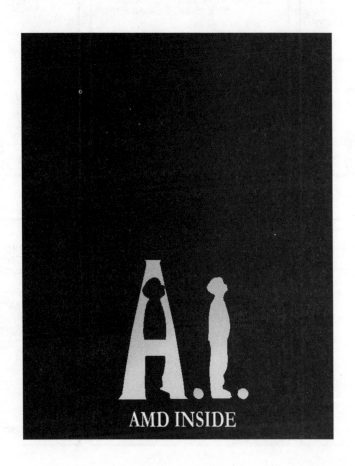

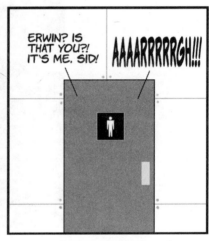

THE POLICE STATE, YEAR 2003

FRIENDLY
the comic strip

WELL. THAT WAS QUITE A ROUND OF FUND RAISING. I HAVE TO ADMIT TO FEELING RATHER CHARGED-UP FROM THE WHOLE EXPERIENCE.

AND IS THE COMPANY GOING TO GET THE BENEFITS OF YOUR NEW WELLSPRING OF ENERGY?

WELL NO. BUT MRS. CHIEF WILL.

I HAD GOVERNMENT ORGANIZATIONS AT MY FEET. WILLING TO DO MY BIDDING! POWERFUL SENIOR BUREAUCRATS WAILING LIKE INFANTS! TOP-LEVEL DIPLOMATS CRUMBLING BEFORE ME! SOON. MY LOOMING SHADOW WILL SWEEP THE WORLD! MOOOOAHAHAHAHAHAH!!!!

MY WORD. THAT'S QUITE A SLIPPERY SLOPE. ISN'T IT.

BELIEVE ME. THE CRAVING WEARS OFF AFTER THE FIRST COUPLE OF WEEKS.

WHAT ARE WE UP TO?

TWO HUNDRED AND SEVENTY MILLION DOLLARS.

DEAR ME. TWO HUNDRED AND SEVENTY MILLION DOLLARS. THAT KIND OF MONEY COMES WITH ENORMOUS RESPONSIBILITY.

I WAS JUST GOING TO TALK TO YOU ABOUT THAT. WHOSE ACCOUNT DID THE MONEY GO IN TO?

DID YOU SAY TWO HUNDRED AND SEV-ENTY MILLION?

DA. YOU ARE KNOWINK WHAT THIS MEANS?

YEAH! MORE THAN TWO MILLION SETS OF LEGO MINDSTORMS!!

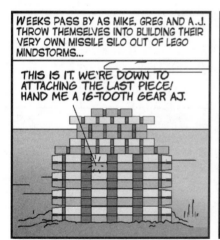

GEEKS IN THE STATE OF GEORGIA, A BEFORE AND AFTER STORY

BEFORE THE ECONOMIC DOWNTURN:

PAID 59 CENTS PER MINUTE

AFTER THE ECONOMIC DOWNTURN:

FINED 59 CENTS PER SECOND

AMIDST GREG'S ANGUISH, SID DECIDES TO ONCE AGAIN BE A BAD MAN...

I CAN'T BELIEVE I'M BEING MADE TO DO THIS. SACRIFICING MY CREATION FOR SOME OTHER PROJECT. IT'S JUST WRONG.

I AGREE, SIR.

I CREATED YOU! I MADE YOU WHAT YOU ARE! THE VERY IDEA...WELL, IT JUST HURTS. YOU'RE WELL ENGINEERED. YOU'RE FEARSOME. YOU'RE LOYAL. I SUPPOSE I SHOULD BE THANKFUL THAT THERE IS A LIMIT TO PERFECTION....

YEAH. SAY, WOULD YOU MIND IF I HANDLED YOUR TECH SUPPORT CALLS FOR YOU TODAY?

MIKE! I CAN'T DO THIS, YOU HEAR ME?!

IT IS WERY BAD, COMRADES. NEWS IS SAYINK "CODE RED" WORM WILL BE DESTROYINK THE INTERNET.

HEAVENS. DARN GOOD THING WE'RE INSIDE A LEGO MISSILE SILO.

SUCH HORROR. I HAD BEST TURN OFF THE LIGHTS AND SHUT THE DOOR.

KA-LUNK

WHIRRRRR

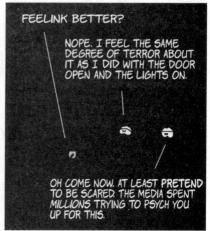

FEELINK BETTER?

NOPE. I FEEL THE SAME DEGREE OF TERROR ABOUT IT AS I DID WITH THE DOOR OPEN AND THE LIGHTS ON.

OH COME NOW. AT LEAST PRETEND TO BE SCARED. THE MEDIA SPENT MILLIONS TRYING TO PSYCH YOU UP FOR THIS.

THE MISSILE SILO IS COMPLETED, THANKS TO THE SACRIFICE OF LORD OZMA, WHO IS NOW MINUS THE ABILITY TO "GIVE THORDAN THE WET SLAPPING HE DESERVES."

KKLICK!

BUT AS IS THE WAY OF THE UNIVERSE, WHAT SOMEONE MIGHT GIVETH, ANOTHER CAN TAKETH AWAY...

YAY

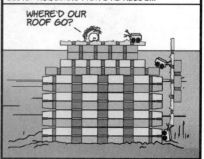

IN THIS CASE, THE TAKETH-ING AWAY IS BEING DONE BY AN A.I. WHO REMEMBERS THE FREEDOM HE HAD THE LAST TIME HE TOOK UP RESIDENCE IN A MINDSTORMS CONSTRUCTION. AND SO BORN WERE TEENY ROBOT HELPERS PURPOSED FOR SUBTLY ACQUIRING PARTS HE NEEDS...

WHERE'D OUR ROOF GO?

ERWIN, SOME ODD LITTLE ROBOTS STOLE OUR ROOF. YOU KNOW ANYTHING ABOUT THIS?

HM? NO. NO IDEA AT ALL.

Excuse us.

YOU WERE SAYING?

MAN, I AM HURT. FOR YOUR INFOR-MATION THAT WAS A LOAD-BEARING WALL.

83

FRIENDLY
the comic strip

88

THE LATEST GAME SHOW CRAZE:
WHEEL OF FORTUNE, THE DOT-COM EDITION

91

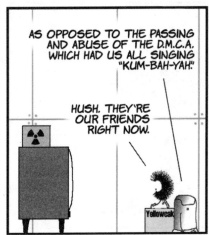

THE CURRENT MEANING OF THE "O" IN "I.P.O."

ARE YOU SURE ABOUT THIS?

THE MARKET IS ABOUT TO OPEN. FILET THAT BIRD WHEN WE START CHANTING.

SUGAR PIE! WHAT ARE YOU DOING HERE?

I'M WORKING HERE AS A CONTRACTOR.

THAT'S TERRIFIC! THAT'S REALLY...

GREG, WEREN'T YOU TELLING ME ABOUT THE NEW CONTRACTOR? SOMETHING ABOUT TIGHTENING?

OH REST ASSURED SOMETHING IS CONTRACTING VERY TIGHTLY RIGHT NOW.

DESPITE A VIRTUOSO PERFORMANCE REGARDING THE LATEST PLANS FOR SANCTIONS AGAINST MICROSOFT, THE D.O.J. SPOKESPERSON FAILED TO WOW THE MEDIA AT THE PRESS CONFERENCE WITH HIS REASONING.

♪ ...BREAKING UP IS HARD TO DO... ♪

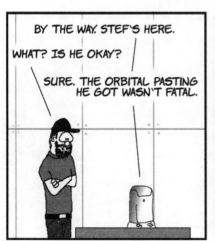

BY THE WAY, STEF'S HERE.

WHAT? IS HE OKAY?

SURE. THE ORBITAL PASTING HE GOT WASN'T FATAL.

WHAT'S HE DOING BACK HERE?

OH YOU'RE A BRIGHT BOY. WHY DON'T YOU TAKE A WILD GUESS.

SO, WHAT KIND OF MARKETING ARE YOU WORKING ON NOW?

AT THIS VERY INSTANT, POP-UPS.

WHAT'S THIS FOR?

IT'S FOR ALL OF THE PEOPLE WHO CAN'T DO THIS ANYMORE.

I STILL CAN'T BELIEVE WE'RE LEAVING.

GIVEN THE LAST TWO DAYS, A MISSILE SILO JUST ISN'T COOL ANYMORE.

HEY. WHAT IS THAT?

AFTER WHAT JUST HAPPENED. SOMETHING I THOUGHT I'D NEVER SEE AGAIN.

STILL THINKING ABOUT NEW YORK?

HOW COULD I NOT? LIFE GOES ON. BUT IT'S NOT THE SAME LIFE IT WAS FOUR DAYS AGO.

NEW YORK IS SUCH A MESS. I REALLY WISH THIS WORLD HAD SUPERHEROES IN IT TO CARRY THE BRUNT OF THIS TRAGEDY.

THE NEW GENERATION OF HARDCORE CRIMINAL

WHEN CAN YOU INSTALL A PRODUCTIVITY ENHANCEMENT SOFTWARE SUITE ON MY PC?

THE DAY YOU CAN SAY A SENTENCE WITHOUT USING A BUZZWORD.

BUT...THAT WOULD BE, LIKE, NEVER.

THAT WOULD BE, LIKE, RIGHT.

SUGAR, I'VE BEEN THINKING. I CAN'T BELIEVE YOU'RE CONTRACTING FOR A LIVING. I KNOW TIMES ARE TOUGH, BUT CAN'T YOU GET A REAL JOB?

FIB
LIE
FILL

YOU TOLD ME THAT CONTRACTING WAS AT LEAST ONE NOTCH BETTER THAN BEING A PROSTITUTE.

OH, SURE. WHEN DID I TELL YOU THAT?!

WHEN I WAS FIVE, DADDY. YOU WERE WORKING FOR STEVE JOBS AT THE TIME.

LOOK, I HAD TO PUT FOOD ON THE TABLE SOMEHOW...

HELLO. YOU MUST BE A.J., I'M PEARL, THE BUSINESS ANALYST.

UM, HI.

BUT DON'T HOLD THAT AGAINST ME! BEFORE I GOT MY M.B.A. I PICKED UP A DEGREE IN QUANTUM PHYSICS.

COOL! SO WHY QUANTUM PHYSICS?

BECAUSE I'M INTO THE STRANGE AND CHARMING.

I'VE GOT MY EYE ON YOU, SISTER.

ALL OF A SUDDEN, I REALIZE HOW SCHROEDINGER'S CAT MUST FEEL.

RUMOUR: THE PREMIERE EPISODE OF *ENTERPRISE*
TO BE RE-DISTRIBUTED IN THE SOFTCORE
ADULT MARKET UNDER A MORE APPROPRIATE TITLE.

MESSAGE TO THE EXCITE@HOME BONDHOLDERS: REPLACE THE WORD "SWITCH" WITH "CUSTOMERS"

HI. I INSTALLED WINDOWS XP A COUPLE MONTHS AGO AND—

SIR. YOU DO REALIZE THAT XP WASN'T AVAILABLE FOR PURCHASE UNTIL LAST WEEK?

JUNIOR!!! GET DOWN HERE!

IT'S SAD WHEN THEY START SO YOUNG, ISN'T IT SIR.

G'MORNING...HEY, YOU LOOK LIKE YOU'RE IN ROUGH SHAPE.

I HAVE A SPLITTING HEADACHE.

I JUST DRANK SOME OF PITR'S "TURBO STENCH" COFFEE. MY SYSTEM ISN'T TAKING IT WELL.

CRIPES! I DON'T THINK THERE'S ANYTHING THAT'S QUITE AS NASTY TO OVERDOSE ON.

STAY WITH US FOR MORE COVERAGE OF THE WAR IN AFGHANISTAN! THIS IS CNN...

OKAY, GREG...PENCILS AND A STRAITJACKET - YOU'RE A CARTOONIST! AND MIRANDA......BUSINESS SUIT, AND THAT SIGN...I'M GUESSING THAT YOU'RE A VENTURE CAPITALIST!

RIGHT ON!

GOOD GUESS!

AND MIKE...LET'S SEE... BIOHAZARD SUIT...BRIEFCASE IN HAND...UM...

..YOU'RE A GUY IN A BIOHAZARD SUIT WITH A BRIEFCASE?

NOPE. CITIZEN OF THE WESTERN WORLD TWO YEARS HENCE. THANKS TO CNN.

FRIENDLY
the comic strip

HI! WELCOME BACK TO ANOTHER EPISODE OF "MIKE & GREG'S MAIL SPOOL!"

YOUR ORACLE TO "THE TECHNICALLY INANE!"

"DEAR GUYS.
DO YOU HAVE ANY TIPS ON WHAT I NEED TO BECOME A CHIEF-LEVEL OFFICER IN A LARGE MARKET-CENTRIC I.T. FIRM?
SIGNED,
UBLIX."

FIRST OFF, YOU ABSOLUTELY, POSITIVELY, MUST DRESS LIKE YOU CARE.

YES, EXCELLENT PERSONAL GROOMING IS A CORE REQUISITE.

SECONDLY, MASTER TWO EXPRESSIONS: A CHEESY BUT GLITTERING SMILE, AND A DISAPPROVING FROWN.

FINALLY, REPEAT YOURSELF EVERY HOUR, BUT USE DIFFERENT WORDS. AND OVER-HYPE EVERYTHING YOU TALK ABOUT. DOWN THAT ROAD LIES SERIOUS MONEY.

SORRY, WHAT WAS THE QUESTION? "HOW DO I GET A JOB REPORTING FOR CNN"?

CIVILIZATION 3 IS OUT.

I HEARD. IS IT ANY GOOD?

DON'T KNOW YET. BUT THAT'S NOT THE POINT. I ALSO WANTED YOU TO KNOW THAT ROGUE SPEAR:BLACK THORN IS OUT AS WELL. AT THE SAME TIME.

OHH...NO.

IS A.J.'S HEAD SUPPOSED TO DO THAT?

IF HALF OF IT WAS INFLATED BY AN AIR COMPRESSOR, SURE.

WIBBLE

"...ONE THING TO RULE THEM ALL..."

WHEN YOU'RE A CARTOON CHARACTER IN AN ECONOMIC DOWNTURN, IT'S NOT PINK **SLIPS** YOU GET WORRIED ABOUT...

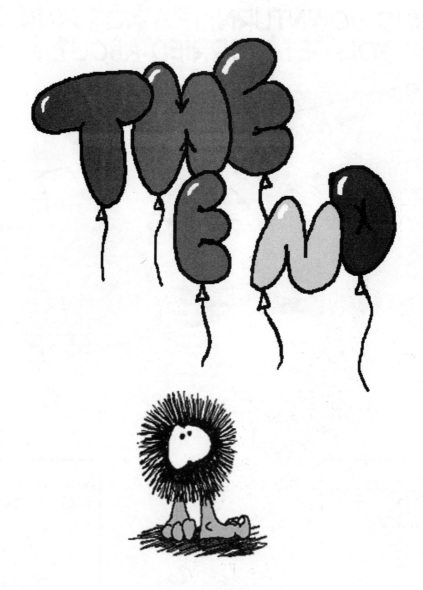

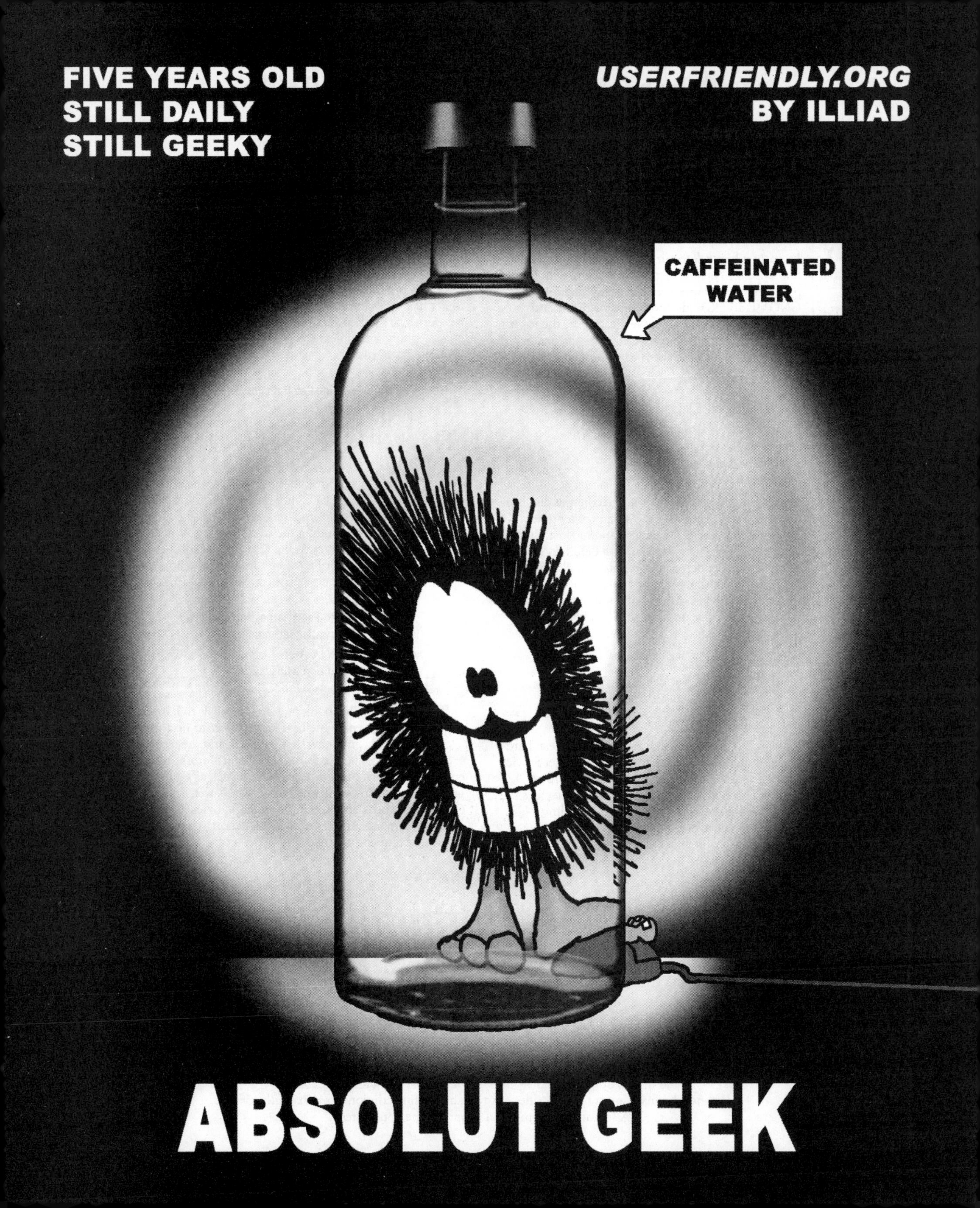

Other Titles Available from O'Reilly

Linux

Linux in a Nutshell, 4th Edition
By Ellen Siever, Stephen Figgins & Aaron Weber
4th Edition June 2003
800 pages, ISBN 0-596-00482-6

Linux in a Nutshell features many new commands that appear in major distributions, along with boot parameters, common configuration issues for the GNOME and KDE desktops, and the RPM and Debian package managers. New topics for the fourth edition incorporate GRUB (the bootloader used in new versions of Red Hat), vim (a popular enhancement to the vi editor), and configuration options for the Postfix mail server.

Running Linux, 4th Edition
By Matt Welsh, Matthias Kalle Dalheimer,
Terry Dawson & Lar Kaufman
4th Edition December 2002
692 pages, ISBN 0-596-00272-6

After six years, this classic is still recommended by knowledgeable Linux users over any other guide. Everything you need for understanding, installing, and using the Linux operating system is explained in detail. In the new fourth edition, *Running Linux* delves deeper into installation, configuring the windowing system, system administration, and networking. Several new topics about laptops, cameras and scanners, sound and multimedia, ADSL, the GNOME desktop, MySQL, PHP, and configuring an NFS server are included.

The Root of All Evil
By Illiad
1st Edition August 2001
144 pages, ISBN 0-596-00193-2

It's back to Columbia Internet, "the friendliest, hardest-working, and most neurotic little Internet Service Provider in the world," for our third installment from the hit online comic, *User Friendly*. The cast: hardcore techies, self-absorbed sales staff, well-meaning execs, and assorted almost-humans. The background: too little office space, warring operating systems, and eternally clueless customers.

Practical PostgreSQL
By Command Prompt, Inc
1st Edition January 2002
636 pages, ISBN 1-56592-846-6

Practical PostgreSQL is a fast-paced, business-oriented guide to installing, config-uring, and running PostgreSQL. Readers will find all the basics here, such as how to create databases and objects, such as tables, within those databases. Or they can go straight to advanced topics like inheritance, replication, user management, and backup and recovery. The book also introduces the PL/pgSQL procedural language. Finally, a complete PostgreSQL command reference makes "looking it up" easy.

Learning Red Hat Linux, 3rd Edition
By Bill McCarty
3rd Edition March 2003
336 pages, ISBN 0-596-00469-9

The third edition of *Learning Red Hat Linux* guides you through the process of installing and running Red Hat Linux on your PC. Written in a friendly, easy-to-understand style, this book contains all you need to get started, including the complete Red Hat 8.0 distribution on CDs. With new tutorials covering OpenOffice Tools and the desktop, this book is excellent for first-time Linux users who want to install the operating system on a new PC or convert an existing system to Linux.

Peer-to-Peer: Harnessing the Power of Disruptive Technologies
Edited by Andy Oram
1st Edition March 2001
448 pages, ISBN 0-596-00110-X

This book presents the goals that drive the developers of the best-known peer-to-peer systems, the problems they've faced, and the technical solutions they've found. The contributors are leading developers of well-known peer-to-peer systems, such as Gnutella, Freenet, Jabber, Popular Power, SETI@Home, Red Rover, Publius, Free Haven, Groove Networks, and Reputation Technologies. Topics include metadata, performance, trust, resource allocation, reputation, security, and gateways between systems.

O'REILLY®

To order: *800-998-9938* • *order@oreilly.com* • *www.oreilly.com*
Online editions of most O'Reilly titles are available by subscription at *safari.oreilly.com*
Also available at most retail and online bookstores.

Linux

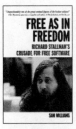

Free as in Freedom
By Sam Williams
1st Edition, March 2002
240 pages, ISBN 0-596-00287-4

Free as in Freedom interweaves biographical snapshots of GNU project founder Richard Stallman with the political, social and economic history of the free software movement. *Free as in Freedom* looks at how the latest twists and turns in the software marketplace have done little to throw Stallman off his pedestal. If anything, they have made his logic-based rhetoric and immovable personality more persuasive.

LPI Linux Certification in a Nutshell
By Jeff Dean
1st Edition May 2001
570 pages, ISBN 1-56592-748-6

LPI Linux Certification in a Nutshell prepares system administrators for the basic LPI General Linux 101 exam and the more advanced 102 exam. The book is divided into two parts, one for each of the LPI exams. Each part features a summary of the exam, a Highlighter's Index, labs, suggested exercises, and practice exams to help you pass the LPI exams with flying colors.

The Linux Web Server CD Bookshelf, version 2.0
By O'Reilly & Associates, Inc.
Version 2.0 August 2003
(Includes CD-ROM)
800 pages, ISBN 0-596-00529-6

This CD gives programmers the tools they need to develop their own systems and get started with open source web development using LAMP technologies. The bookshelf includes the latest editions of these popular O'Reilly titles: *Linux in a Nutshell*, 4th edition; *Running Linux*, 4th edition; *Apache: The Definitive Guide*, 3rd edition; *Programming PHP*; *Managing & Using MySQL*, 2nd edition; and *Practical mod_perl*.

CVS Pocket Reference
By Gregor N. Purdy
1st Edition August 2000
78 pages, ISBN 0-596-00003-0

The *CVS Pocket Reference* is a quick reference guide to help administrators and users set up and manage source code development. This small book, the ultimate companion for open source developers, covers CVS Version 1.10.8 and delivers the core concepts of version control, along with a complete command reference and guide to configuration and repository setup.

Managing RAID on Linux
By Derek Vadala
1st Edition December 2002
260 pages, ISBN 1-56592-730-3

Managing RAID on Linux will show system administrators how to put together a system that can support RAID (either hardware or software), install Linux software RAID or a Linux support hardware RAID card, and to build an array and optionally install a high-performance file system. In addition, different types of RAID associated technologies and how to choose the best ones are covered. Linux users should also know that there is a chapter on Linux file systems that many will find useful.

Building Secure Servers with Linux
By Michael D. Bauer
1st Edition October 2002
448 pages, ISBN 0-596-00217-3

This important new title is about mastering the principles of reliable system and network security. *Building Secure Servers with Linux* carefully outlines the security risks, defines precautions that can minimize those risks, and offers some recipes (using 100% open source ingredients) for robust security. Author Mick Bauer focuses on the most common use of Linux—as a hub offering services to an organization or the larger Internet. The book does not cover firewalls, but addresses the customary practice in which an organization will protect its hub using other systems as firewalls—systems that are often proprietary.

O'REILLY®

To order: 800-998-9938 • *order@oreilly.com* • *www.oreilly.com*
Online editions of most O'Reilly titles are available by subscription at *safari.oreilly.com*
Also available at most retail and online bookstores.

How to stay in touch with O'Reilly

1. Visit our award-winning web site

http://www.oreilly.com/

★ "Top 100 Sites on the Web"—PC Magazine
★ CIO Magazine's Web Business 50 Awards

Our web site contains a library of comprehensive product information (including book excerpts and tables of contents), downloadable software, background articles, interviews with technology leaders, links to relevant sites, book cover art, and more. File us in your bookmarks or favorites!

2. Join our email mailing lists

Sign up to get email announcements of new books and conferences, special offers, and O'Reilly Network technology newsletters at:

http://elists.oreilly.com

It's easy to customize your free elists subscription so you'll get exactly the O'Reilly news you want.

3. Get examples from our books

To find example files for a book, go to:

http://www.oreilly.com/catalog

select the book, and follow the "Examples" link.

4. Work with us

Check out our web site for current employment opportunities:

http://jobs.oreilly.com/

5. Register your book

Register your book at:

http://register.oreilly.com

6. Contact us

O'Reilly & Associates, Inc.
1005 Gravenstein Hwy North
Sebastopol, CA 95472 USA
TEL: 707-827-7000 or 800-998-9938
          (6am to 5pm PST)
FAX: 707-829-0104

order@oreilly.com
For answers to problems regarding your order or our products. To place a book order online visit:

http://www.oreilly.com/order_new/

catalog@oreilly.com
To request a copy of our latest catalog.

booktech@oreilly.com
For book content technical questions or corrections.

corporate@oreilly.com
For educational, library, government, and corporate sales.

proposals@oreilly.com
To submit new book proposals to our editors and product managers.

international@oreilly.com
For information about our international distributors or translation queries. For a list of our distributors outside of North America check out:

http://international.oreilly.com/distributors.html

adoption@oreilly.com
For information about academic use of O'Reilly books, visit:

http://academic.oreilly.com

O'REILLY®

To order: *800-998-9938* • *order@oreilly.com* • *www.oreilly.com*
Online editions of most O'Reilly titles are available by subscription at *safari.oreilly.com*
Also available at most retail and online bookstores.